Presented to

_____

from

_____

_____

_____ _19___

Other Books in the
Children of the King Series:

The King's Alphabet
A Bible Book About Letters

The King's Numbers
A Bible Book About Counting

The King's Manners
A Bible Book About Courtesy

The King's Workers
A Bible Book About Serving

The King's Animals
A Bible Book About God's Creatures

Managing Editor: Laura Minchew
Project Editor: Brenda Ward

The King's Children
Copyright © 1991 by WORD Publishing

Library of Congress Cataloging-in-Publication Data

Hollingsworth, Mary, 1947-
The King's children : a Bible book about God's people / illustrated by
Mary Grace Eubank : text by Mary Hollingsworth.
p. cm. — (The Children of the King series)
"Word kids!"
Summary: Rhyming text depicts the children of the world from
Africa to Greece to the United States and describes the God who
created them all.
ISBN 0-8499-0906-6
1: Children — Juvenile literature. 2. Children — Religious life —
Juvenile literature. 3. Creation — Juvenile literature. [1. Children–
Religious life. 2. Christian life.] I. Eubank, Mary Grace, ill. II.
Title. III. Series: Hollingsworth, Mary, 1947-
Children of the King series.
HQ781.H76 1991
305.23 — dc20   91-19092
                                                                              CIP
                                                                              AC
Printed in the United States of America
12349LB987654321

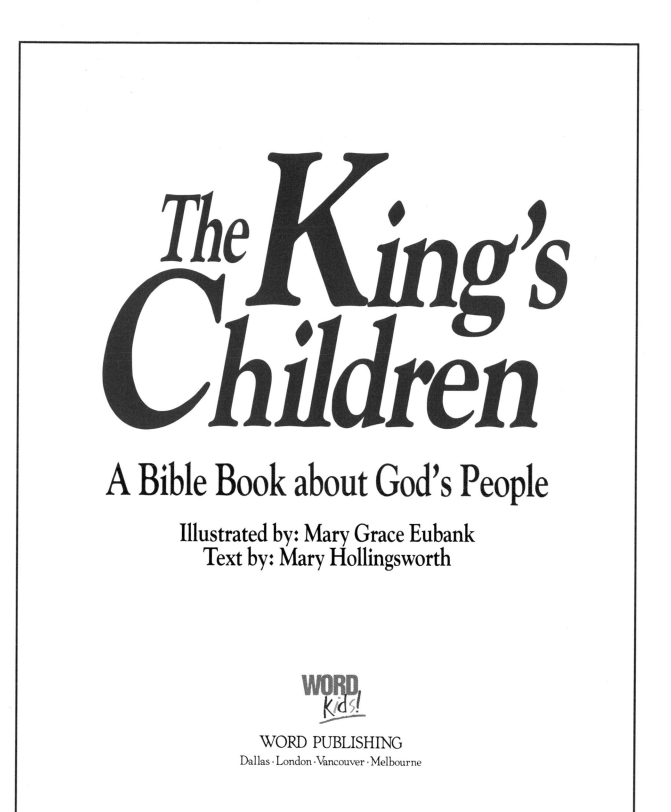

The King's Children

A Bible Book about God's People

Illustrated by: Mary Grace Eubank
Text by: Mary Hollingsworth

WORD *kids!*

WORD PUBLISHING
Dallas · London · Vancouver · Melbourne

Dear Parents,

A strong family heritage is very important to pass on to our children. It gives them a sense of belonging and pride. *The King's Children* teaches that people of every race and culture have a wonderful, unique heritage. Children will learn not only to respect their own background, but the background of others as well.

While the dress styles in the book are not necessarily adopted by modern children in each of these countries, they will illustrate the originality of each country and its people. And you'll notice on the last page that the king is embracing modern children from all nationalities.

In a world that urges children to conform, this book says celebrate who you are and the extraordinary characteristics that make you unique . . . and celebrate with others the differences and similarities that make them special.

The Publisher

The King looked 'round at every place,
And the frown ran away from His face.
In every land and every place
His children were showing His grace.

Australia

Some Aussies' homes are outback ranches
Where koalas enjoy eucalyptus branches.
Their friends are sheep and kangaroo.
"G'day, Mate," is how they welcome you.

Brazil

Rio de Janeiro
Is a city where you'd like to go.
You'll hear a welcome in Portuguese
And feel a nice, cool ocean breeze.

Canada

Pierre's at home in Canada
Where the waters fall free at Niagara.
With giant moose and grizzly bear,
This land shows God's wonderful care.

China

Chen Li's small house is in Bejing
Where trees flower out in the spring.
With chopsticks Chen eats rice and fish,
And his rickshaw will go where you wish.

Egypt

Talil lives near a pyramid
(Where Joseph was sold as a kid).
He goes to shop the town bazaar
On his camel, not in a big car.

France

"Parlez vous français?" they say
When you visit François' small chalet.
Vineyards, mountains, a sidewalk cafe—
Yes, God really blessed France, I'd say.

Germany

In Germany Klaus and his brother Von
Ride with their dad on the Autobahn.
They see cathedrals in every place
Where children learn of God's rich grace.

India

In India stands the Taj Mahal—
A palace so lovely and tall.
Saba rides his ox-drawn cart,
Bringing his goods to the mart.

Ireland

Patrick runs through dale and glen
With his happy Irish setter, Ben.
God smiles and looks around with pride
At His clover-covered countryside.

Israel

Aaron says, "Shalom, my friend,"
As he kindly escorts you on in.
Hebrew is the language heard—
It's the language of God's holy Word.

Italy

Stefano feels right at home
In his bakery shop in old Rome.
Pastas are his favorite meals,
And he thanks God as he kneels.

Japan

Yoko greets you at the door
And invites you to sit on the floor.
She serves you fish and fresh green tea.
Her kimono's so pretty to see.

Kenya

Kenya is Kadula's home,
Where animals happily roam.
In cities, plains and jungle lands
God's people obey His commands.

Korea

Seoul, Korea is where Kim Lee
Skates with her friend named Su Kee.
Soccer, hiking and Tai Kwan Do
Are their favorite sports, don't you know?

Mexico

"Hola," Pedro says and smiles,
As he tips his sombrero with style.
Tortillas, rice and beans taste great;
So, at dinnertime, don't you be late!

Netherlands

Windmills go around and 'round
In Helga and Nils' happy town.
They play in noisy wooden shoes,
'Midst tulips of yellows and blues.

Peru

"Buenos dias," Rosa greets,
And she offers you sweet, tasty treats—
Bananas, corn and sugar cane
Are grown in the jungle and the plain.

New Zealand

Errol picks up paua shells
For jewelry his family sells.
New Zealand is his native home,
Where God's kiwi and wallaby roam.

Philippines

Lanna's house is by the seas
And cooled by the gentle salt breeze.
She eats fresh coconut and fish
And chocolate—
what more could you wish?

Russia

"Brrr!" laughs little Russian Ivan,
Running as fast as he can.
He raises reindeer that are tame,
And ice hockey's his favorite game.

Singapore

On the island of Singapore,
Puck Dee plays all day on the shore.
He loves to catch a string of fish,
And following God is his wish.

South Africa

Jacob's from South Africa—
Home of the ostrich and cheetah,
Mines of diamonds and gold,
And Victoria Falls, big and bold.

Spain

Juan's a happy Spanish boy,
Who worships our God with great joy.
He waves his cape and shouts, "Ole!"
For bullfight's a fun game to play.

Sweden

Sven and Ingrid's home in Sweden
Is just like the Garden of Eden,
Where lumberjacks cut down big trees,
And dairies make butter and cheese.

United Kingdom

A thatch-roofed cottage on the Thames,
A visit to see royal gems,
Trifle, biscuits, scones and tea
Make Margaret happy, you see.

United States

"Hello," says Bobby, smiling wide,
As he asks you to come on outside
For hot dogs, sodas, chips or fries,
And a big piece of Mom's apple pie.

The King touched every tiny head,
Whether yellow, black, white, brown or red.
And He blessed each child of every race
With His kindness, deep love and sweet grace.